INDIGENOUS FAMILIES: LIFE IN HARMONY WITH NATURE

NORTHWATER

CONSTANTINE ISSIGHOS

Copyright 2013 © Constantine Issighos. Published in Canada. Printed in U.S.A. No part of this book may be reproduced or transmitted in any form or by any means, electronic or mechanical, including photocopying, recording, and/or by any information storage and retrieval system except by a reviewer who may quote brief passages in a review to be printed in a magazine, newspaper, or on the web without written permission in writing from the author/publisher. For information, please contact www.awaqkunabooks.com

NorthWater is an imprint of Awaqkuna Books Inc.

Vol. 16 Of THE AMAZON EXPLORATION SERIES:
THE CALL OF THE SHAMANS

Library and Archives Canada

ISBN 978-0-9878601-6-3

Library and Archives Canada Cataloguing in Publication

ATTENTION CHILDRENS ASSOCIATIONS, BOOK STORES, PUBLIC OR PRIVATE LIBRARIES: quantity discounts are available on bulk purchases of this book series.

THE AMAZON EXPLORATION SERIES
Children's Books
by
Constantine Issighos

1. Upper Amazon Voyage by River Boat
2. The People of the River
3. The Children of the River
4. Amazon's Nature of Things
5. Echoes of Nature: a Beautiful Wild Habitat
6. The Amazon Rainforest
7. Amazonian Sisterhood
8. Amazon River Wolves
9. Amazonian Landscapes and Sunsets
10. Amazonian Canopy: the Roof of the World's Rainforest
11. Amazonian Tribes: a World of Difference
12. Birds and Butterflies of the Amazon
13. The Great Wonders of the Amazon
14. The Jaguar People
15. The Fresh Water Giants
16. The Call of the Shamans
17. Indigenous Families: Life in Harmony with Nature
18. Amazon in Peril
19. Giant Tarantulas and Centipes
20. Amazon Ethnobotanical Garden
21. Amazon Tribal Warrios

The Environment

The Amazon of the past is one of the great mysteries needing further exploration science. In this unknown past lie the origins of the biodiversity of the richest eco-system on Earth. What is known, however, is that 15 million years ago the South America plate collided with the Nazca plate. This gave rise to the Andean mountain range to form a linkage of the Brazilian and Guyana bedrock shields. This linkage blocked the flow of the Amazon River, causing it to become a vast inland sea.

In the next several million years, gradually the inland sea became a massive swampy, freshwater lake and the marine life adapted to life in freshwater. In time, the forest dried out, species that were once one had diversified enough to be designated as separate species and the Amazon Lake drained and became a river.

Tribal Communities

The Amazon rainforest has a long history of indigenous settlement. These communities achieved a sustainable balance in their unique eco-systems. Unlike those using current cultivation techniques, the Amazonian communities were aware of the ecological realities of their environment which came from 5,000 years of trial and error on how to sustainably manage the rainforest to suit their needs.

The Amazonian tribal system is made up of about 200 tribal groups. Depending on the area in which they live and the particular Amazon tribe to which they belong, they have had various degrees of influence from outside cultures. This is an obvious fact, since the Amazon rainforest geography is divided among 9 different countries: Bolivia, Brazil, Colombia, Ecuador, French Guyana, Guyana, Peru, Suriname and Venezuela.

The traditional village structure is a circle of thatched-roof huts around a large man-made circular clearing, which serves as the men's meeting place. Men of the village meet in the central hut; the huts on the periphery are considered women's domain. The thatched-roof huts are quite roomy and large enough for an entire family. There are no mattresses; bedding usually consists of hammocks. They are much cooler, since air flows around them, and are

more comfortable (as I discovered) in a jungle environment.
Other tribes such as the Yanomani live in communal settings where members of a group form extended families. In such a communal living style, the Yanomani help each other to make it through life; sharing is vital to their survival.

Extended Family Life
A Yanomani village structure consists of zones arranged in concentric circles. The large communal house is at the center of the village clearing, where most of the cultural activities are held. Its internal division is also made up of circular sections where the communal meals are cooked. It also serves as a visiting and festival space. At night it becomes a sleeping room for the young single men. A secondary space around it is further divided into walled sections for individual families within the extended family.
The spatial organization of the village consists of work huts, one per extended family. These are small huts with no walls and with a thatched two-slope roof. It is where women sew, weave, cook or scrape manioc. Men may use a space within these huts only to fix their hunting and fishing tools.

Subsistence
On the outside periphery of each village there are small gardens or plots, one per each extended family, where women cultivate vegetables, tobacco, medicinal plants, sugarcane and cotton. In this way the indigenous women maintain their food traditions and their way of producing this food. Much of the fruits still grow wild in the jungle, which explains why fruit is so vital to the villager's diet. Women collect forest fruits such as bananas, pineapples, avocados, mangos, and a variety of greens to supplement their family's diet. It is estimated that indigenous people have names for 55 different fruit trees; only a few have a scientific name, such as the Brazil nut or the acai. In addition to food, they also utilize forest plants for medicine.
Men are basically hunters, fishermen and gatherers. Hunting is an integral part of many Amazonian communities. To hunt, men use homemade poison-dipped darts, spears, blowpipes, and bows and

arrows. The indigenous men carry their bows and arrows with them at all times. Many sleep with them as well in order to have quick access to them. These bows and arrows are used for hunting, fishing, protection and warfare. Another means of hunting is trapping. Traps, however, are not only for hunting; they are set up also as a defence during warfare.

Since the indigenous people are completely dependent on the jungle, they have a deep sense of connection to their ecology.

Trade amongst Tribes
Hundreds of years ago in the Amazon rainforest, indigenous people carried on a way of life similar to how they live in isolation today. That is, a world without money, a world without any form of monetary exchange or currency. They used a process of exchange of goods for goods. The primary mode of exchange between extended families or tribes was bartering. The most common way to barter is to trade for goods. No bartering for "services" exists, since the notion of "services" is a western concept, not an indigenous one.

From the ancient Amazonian tribes, and what we know of their culture, we can conclude how fundamental this system of bartering still is today. During bartering, social prestige and profit is irrelevant amongst the barterers. Bartering is viewed as a way not only of obtaining needed goods but also as an important mechanism of strengthening relationships within the tribe's extended families and within neighbouring communities.

Gender Roles
According to early legends recorded by the explorer Francisco de Orellana in 1542, some of the most violent natives in the Amazon were women warriors. Women warriors appeared to be on the frontlines in the confrontation between the explorers and the natives. These legends contributed by the Greek myth-inspired name of the warrior women and Orellana ultimately named the area, Amazonas. The original Amazon myth was started by the Sicilian historian Diodorous who in the second century B.C., introduced the story of the women warriors, Amazonas. The Amazon region was located on the

coast of North Africa, which was reigned by a gynaecocracy, which means, that only women were qualified to join the warrior class. The region was ruled by a Queen Myrina. Her army consisted of 30,000 female foot soldiers and 3,000 cavalry. Queen Myrina successfully confronted a number of male armies along the coast of North Africa. In a final battle, the Queen Myrina fell and her brave female soldiers scattered.

Today's Amazon is occupied by different tribes, where, for both sexes, nudity is nothing to be ashamed of. In the Cambeba, the Yanomani, the Piraha and other tribes as well, men and women go about their daily tasks naked—except for a small apron for women—without feeling uncomfortable being seen by outsiders.

Most Amazonian tribes are patriarchical and life in some tribes is more difficult for women than in others. Tribes such as the Cumbeba, the Yanomani and the Piraha in the Northwest Amazon maintain a hard line for women. While men work intermittently, women have round-the-clock work as mothers, keepers of the house and they are also responsible for the majority of the agricultural tasks. All of these tasks are done with the babies on their backs, even when they are collecting forest fruits and greens. In addition, women are expected to help men and be responsible for the production of all non-meat foods. In intimate relationships the concepts of romance, romantic courtship and romantic love-making is not actually considered.

Men are warriors and hunters and any work beyond that is done by women.

The Children of the Amazon

The Amazon rainforest is occupied by hundreds of tribes rich in individuality and distinct cultures. Most of the tribes are isolated and remain as independent entities, with little or no exposure to cultures beyond their own. Children that are raised within these tribes are very dependent on the family elders; they learn to co-operate as one with the environment to ensure the success and longevity of the tribe.

Children do not have a very long childhood compared to what we—in the western world—consider growing up years. By the age of ten children are expected to work as hard as the adults. They do not have any choice in the matter. In fact, in the Piraha tribe, children are responsible to take care of themselves as soon as they are able to walk around. It is the Piraha's way of toughening up their children. Mothers do not tell their children fairytales, nor do they paint or do any sort of crafts with their children—actually nobody tells any kinds of stories.

In Amazonian riverbank communities, children by the age of 6 are expected to transport traded goods by canoe to other communities. Seeing children canoeing alone on the Amazon River is a common sight.

Socializing

You may wonder how the indigenous people, young and not so young, entertain themselves without videos, Internet, computer games, movies and TV sitcoms. The answer is simple: entertainment is a communal affair that involves nearly everyone in the village. Almost all of the tribes have one or more storytellers. It is a tradition that it is as ancient as the tribes themselves. During the storytelling, any member may participate in the entertainment. There is no written script, nor is there a director, for the entertainment is spontaneous. The participants, including the head storyteller, uses techniques that include pantomime, repetition, mimicry and the re-enactment of animal sounds involved in the story. Some of the participants are greatly skilled storytellers who re-enact tribal legends. These are passed down from generation to generation through the oral tradition of storytelling.

A major part of socialising is invitations between tribes to share in a festival. The host tribe provides hospitality, which includes the roasting of pigs, monkeys or birds, a variety of fruits and homemade drinks. Members from the invited village travel a long way by canoe to attend such a ceremony. A reciprocal invitation is offered to the host village, and this repeated social exchange strengthens relations between communities.

Spirituality
Rituals and Ceremonies

As with most indigenous communities, there is a shared belief that there is a visible world, an underworld and heaven. These beliefs are rooted in the influence of the Christian missionaries who penetrated the indigenous communities in order to convert them with their religious dogma. Original spiritual concepts are still part of the indigenous mentality. Daily life on earth is mixed with the influence from the great beyond and the living co-exists with the spirits of their ancestors.

The Amazon jungle provides indigenous people with the mystical and the necessary natural resources for their ceremonies and rituals. They use diverse material such as, precious stones, bird feathers, seashells, and dyes for painting their bodies, and medicinal plants for making drinks associated with symbolic power and values.

The Ashanikas tribe of the southern Amazon, however, observe a far more complex spirituality. Their shamanistic cosmological system divides the universe into various levels that clearly define the boundaries between Good and Evil.

Arts and Crafts

Art is not just for visual entertainment; art transmits meaning and tells a story for the indigenous people. The artistic value put into pottery or basket weaving is passed down from one generation to the next. Art within the Amazonian tribes is inspired from many aspects of daily life, such as the relationship between humans and animals, or the commemoration of an event. Artwork designs have become more intricate as demand for them has increased.

The Yecuana tribe of the Venezuela region of the Amazon weave baskets reminiscent of the North American Cherokee's basketry. They use a variety of natural dyes to create colour and contrast. The designs on the flat serving baskets are made by men; they are the "cosmograms" of their universe, not only models of the flat hemisphere and of the dome of the heavens, but also circular fields representing atmospheric elements.

Constantine Issighos   The Amazon Exploration Series

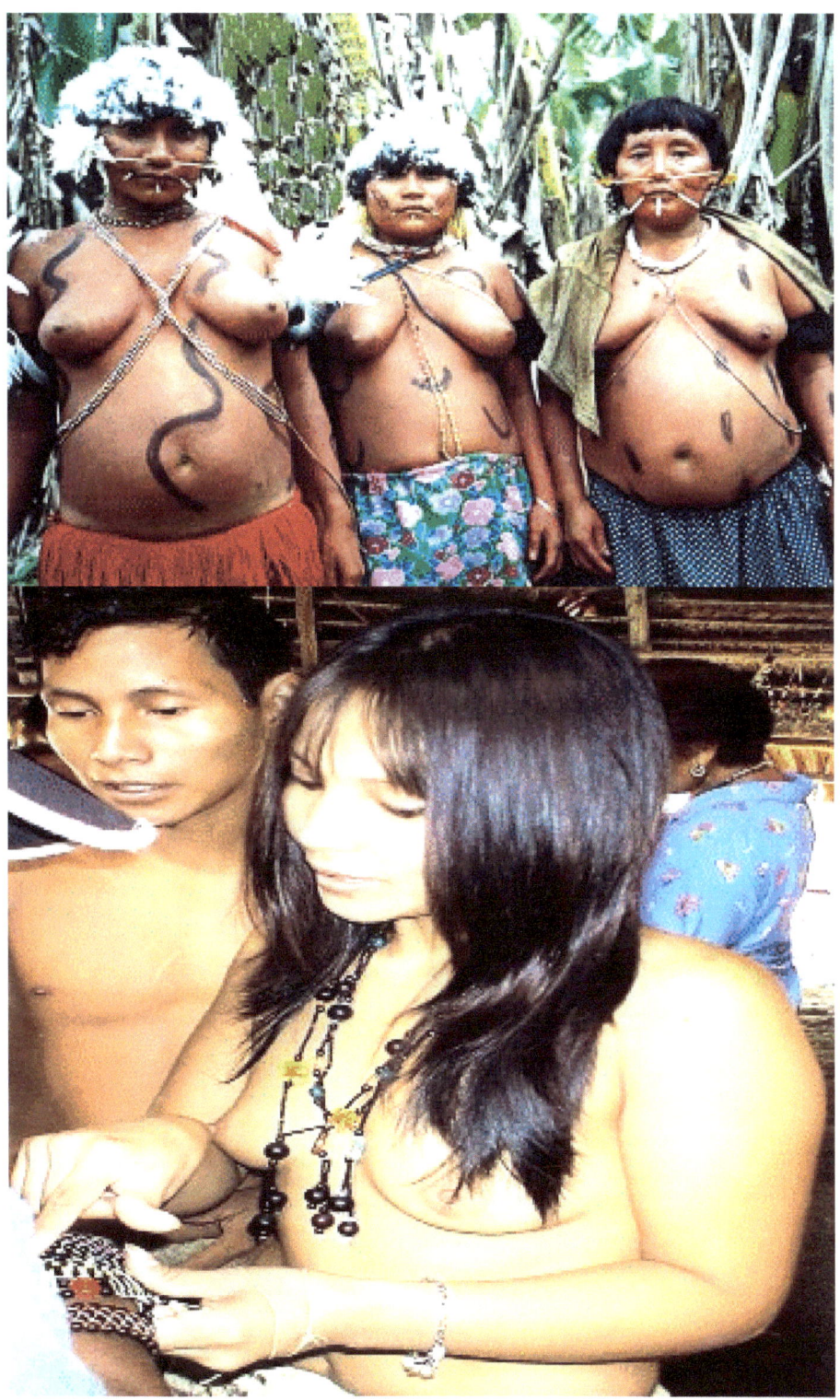

INDIGENOUS FAMILIES

The Amazon Exploration Series — Constantine Issighos

INDIGENOUS FAMILIES

The Amazon Exploration Series — Constantine Issighos

INDIGENOUS FAMILIES

Constantine Issighos　　　　　　The Amazon Exploration Series

INDIGENOUS FAMILIES

The Amazon Exploration Series — Constantine Issighos

INDIGENOUS FAMILIES

Constantine Issighos The Amazon Exploration Series

The Amazon Exploration Series — Constantine Issighos

INDIGENOUS FAMILIES

The Amazon Exploration Series — Constantine Issighos

INDIGENOUS FAMILIES

Constantine Issighos		The Amazon Exploration Series

25		INDIGENOUS FAMILIES

The Amazon Exploration Series — Constantine Issighos

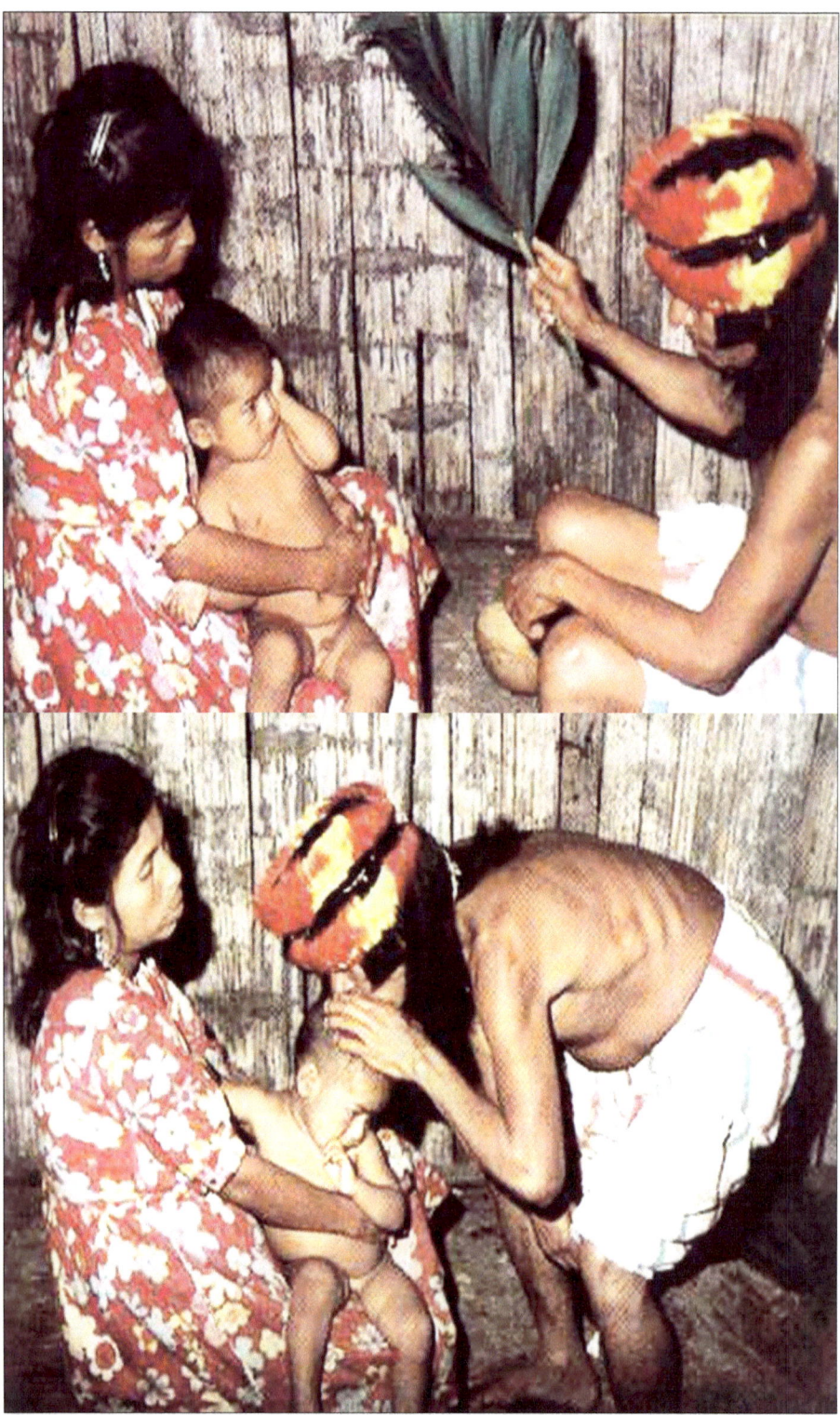

INDIGENOUS FAMILIES

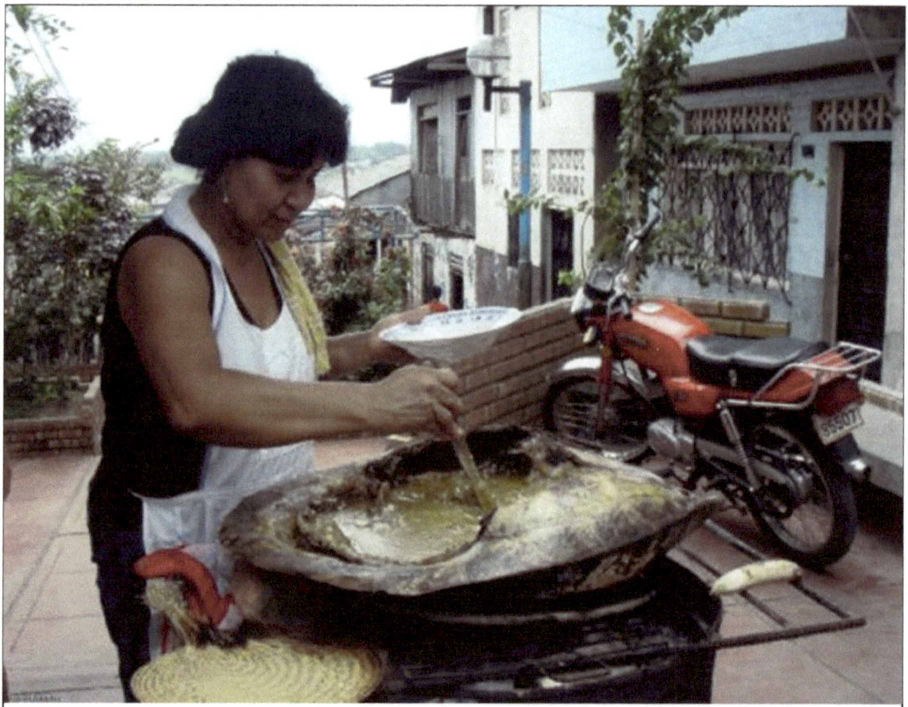

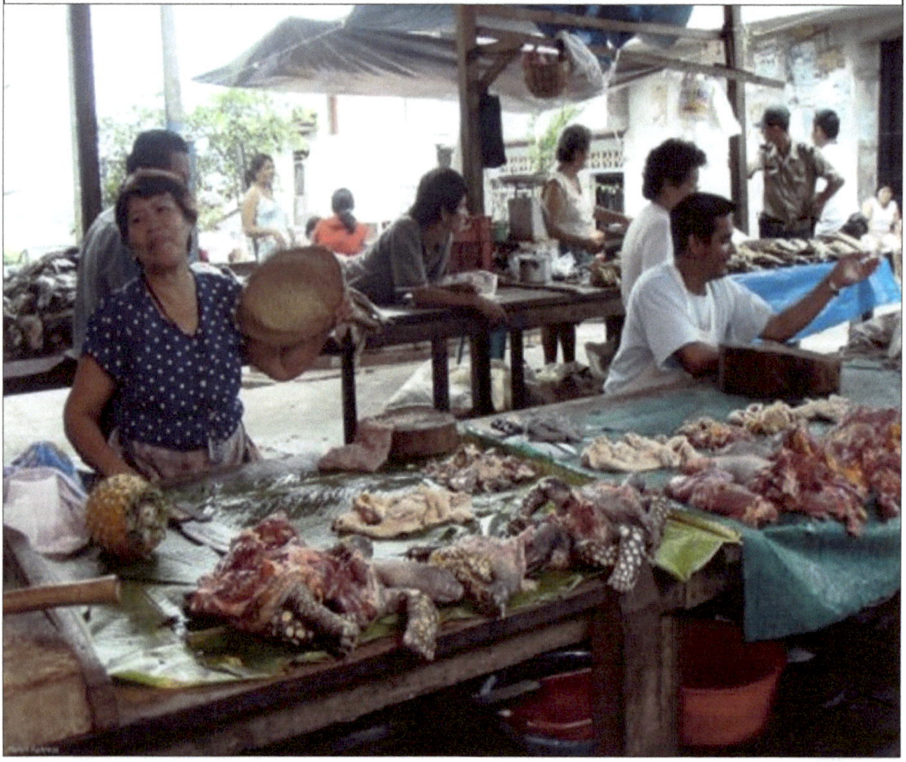

The Amazon Exploration Series — Constantine Issighos

INDIGENOUS FAMILIES

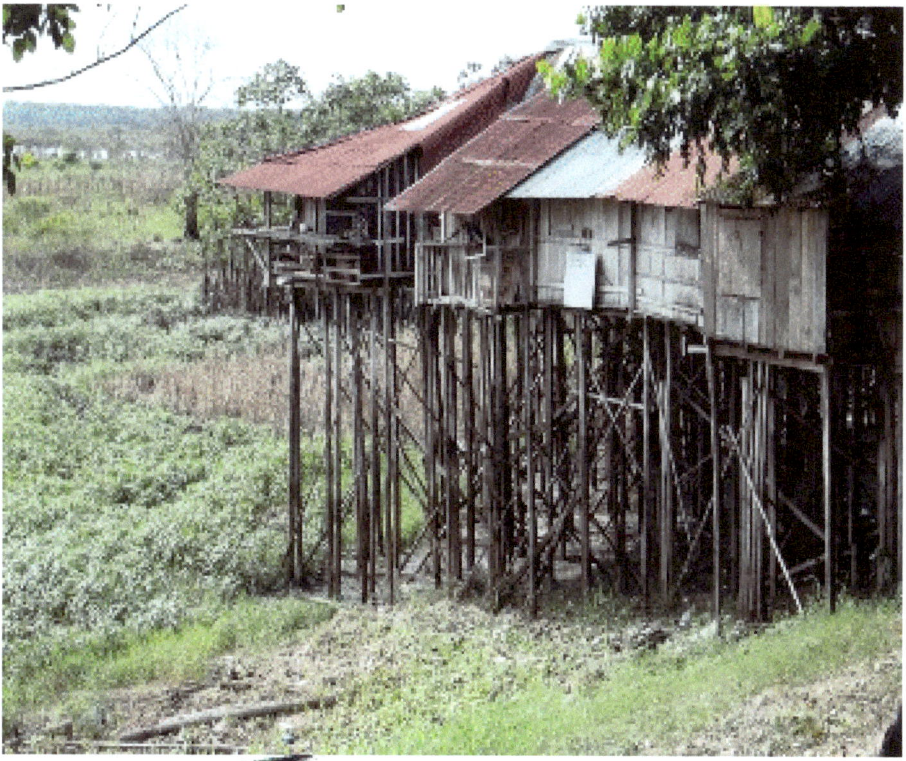

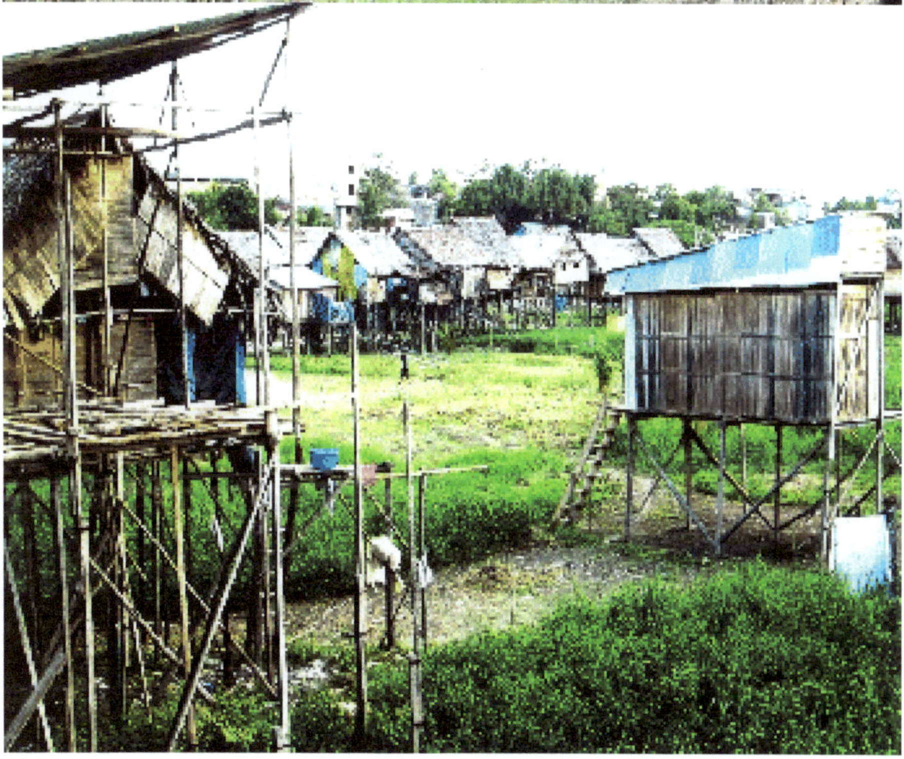

The Amazon Exploration Series   Constantine Issighos

INDIGENOUS FAMILIES   32

Constantine Issighos The Amazon Exploration Series

INDIGENOUS FAMILIES

The Amazon Exploration Series   Constantine Issighos

INDIGENOUS FAMILIES   34

The Amazon Exploration Series   Constantine Issighos

INDIGENOUS FAMILIES   36

Constantine Issighos   The Amazon Exploration Series

37   INDIGENOUS FAMILIES

The Amazon Exploration Series   Constantine Issighos

INDIGENOUS FAMILIES

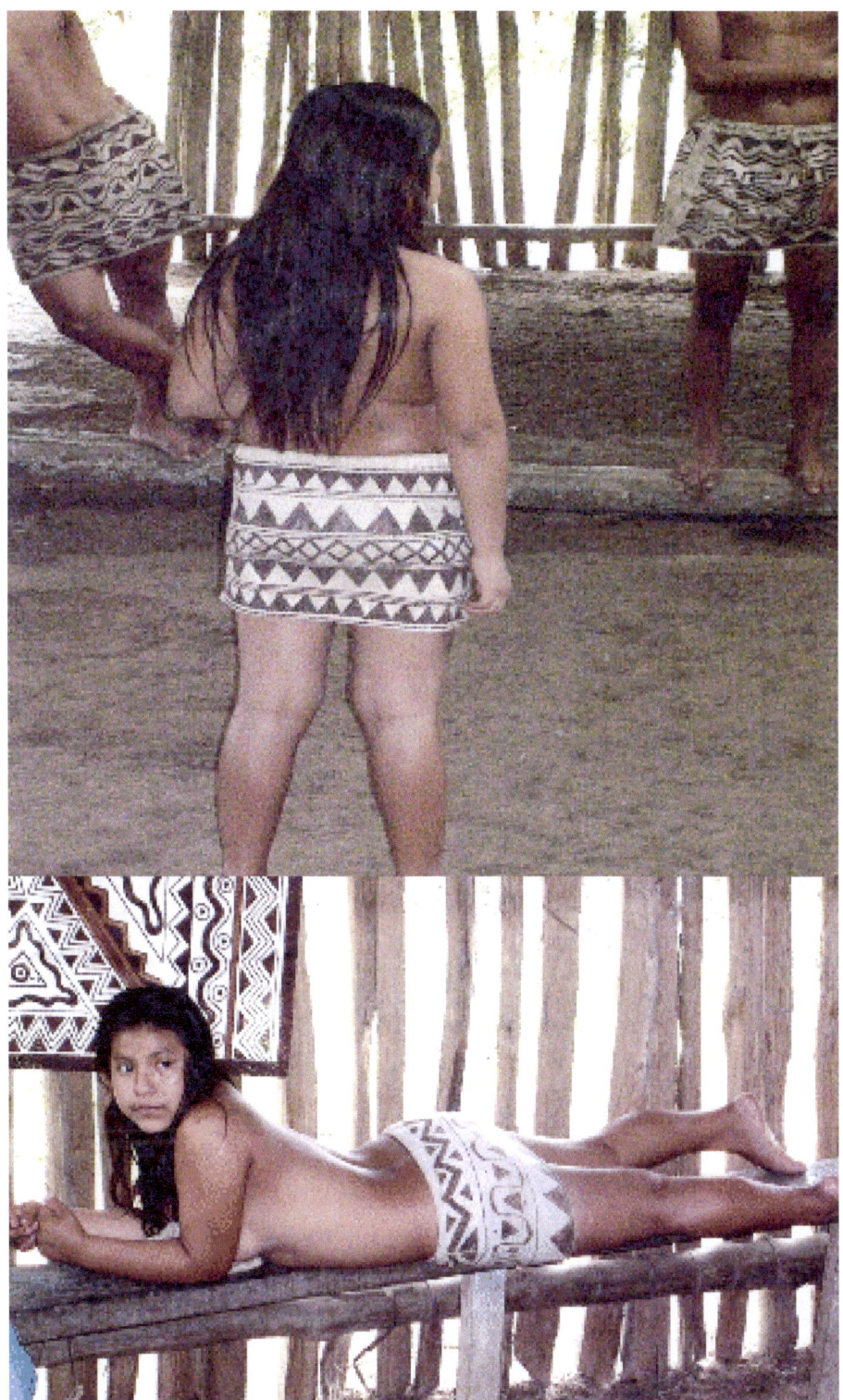

The Amazon Exploration Series   Constantine Issighos

INDIGENOUS FAMILIES

Constantine Issighos   The Amazon Exploration Series

INDIGENOUS FAMILIES

The Amazon Exploration Series   Constantine Issighos

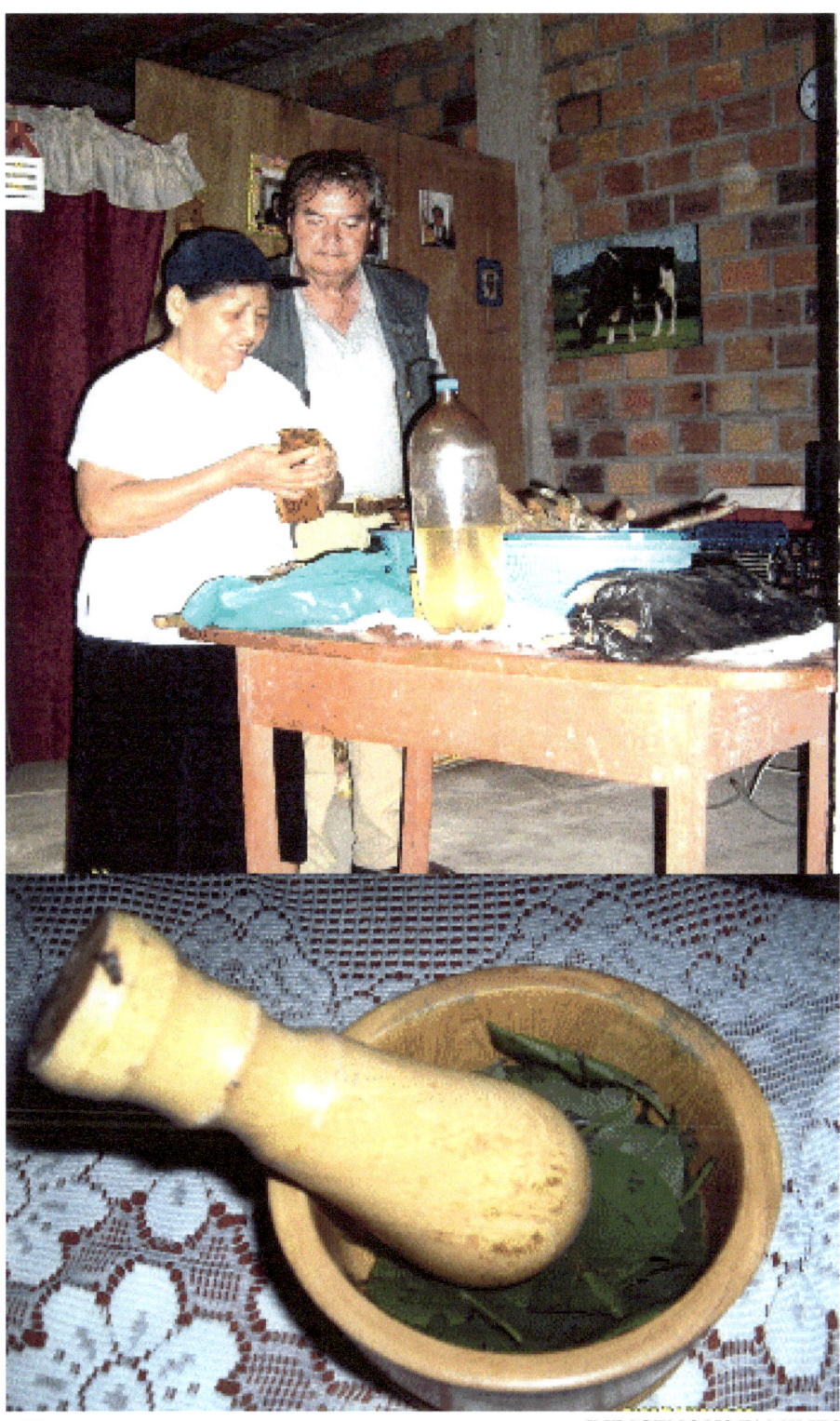

The Amazon Exploration Series Constantine Issighos

INDIGENOUS FAMILIES 48

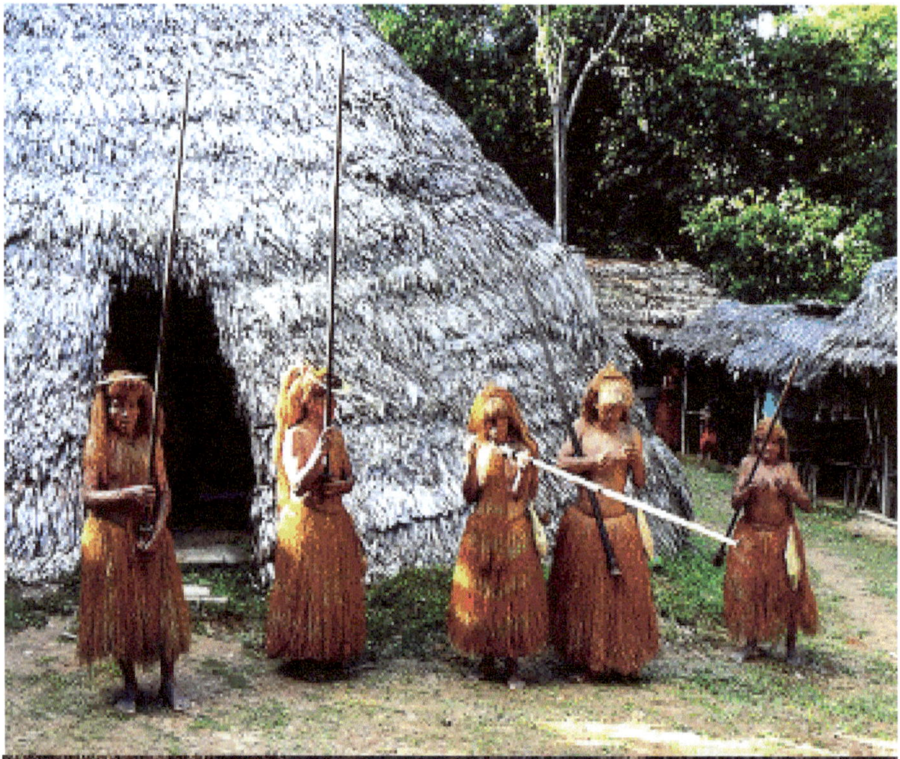

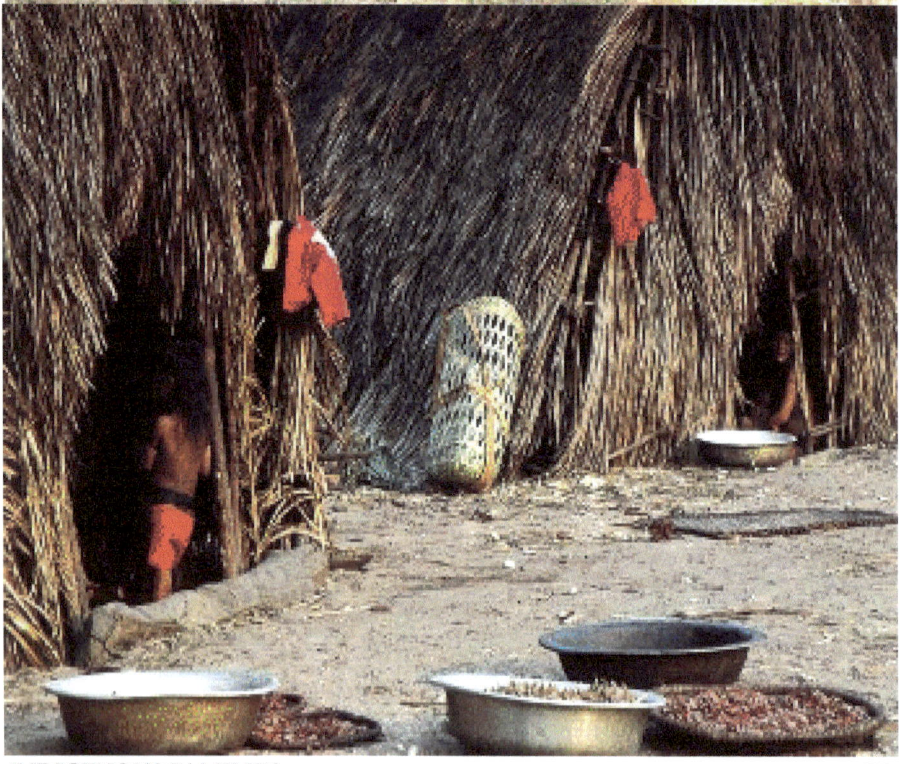

www.ingramcontent.com/pod-product-compliance
Lightning Source LLC
Chambersburg PA
CBHW041753040426
42446CB00001B/23